Schott New York

Tobias Picker
b.1954

ARIAS
for Tenor and Piano

Edited by
Samuel Bill
Juan Pablo Contreras
Scott Wollschleger

ED 30135

www.schott-music.com

Mainz · London · Madrid · New York · Paris · Prague · Tokyo · Toronto
© 2014 SCHOTT HELICON MUSIC CORPORATION, New York · Printed in USA

Contents

Foreword

When it comes to American opera, we are living in the middle of a Renaissance — or a boom, if you will, since the intensity of creative activity devoted to composing and producing new operas has no real precedent in this country. Tobias Picker has been a major part of this Renaissance over the past two decades, from the moment he launched his career as an opera composer with *Emmeline* at Santa Fe Opera.

It's far from usual, with one's first attempt at this complex, interdependent, hybrid genre, to hit the kind of home run Mr. Picker achieved. Yet he had wisely taken his time before embarking on *Emmeline*. A creative prodigy, Mr. Picker spent the first decades of his career developing a distinctive voice in his orchestral, chamber, and solo compositions — and honing compositional skills that have informed every aspect of his writing for the stage.

It wasn't until he'd reached the age of 40 that creative urge and circumstance converged in a commission to set Judith Rossner's novel about Emmeline Mosher, a fictionalized account of a real-life nineteenth-century woman and her grimly tragic fate. But since then Mr. Picker has produced a catalogue of five substantial operas — not to mention chamber versions of several of these to enable performances by smaller companies and a major new revision of *An American Tragedy* for its revival at the 2014 Glimmerglass Festival.

Because so much of his subject matter centers on the passions and emotional turmoil of ordinary people caught up in realistic, unforgiving situations, Mr. Picker's operatic style was soon branded "American verismo." As far as such comparisons go, he says he doesn't mind, even finding this a compliment, though it says nothing about his music itself — beyond the fact that each of his operas is seamlessly structured to allow for the heightened moments of revelation to which arias and varied ensembles are so well suited.

By collaborating with such gifted librettists as the poet J.D. McClatchy and Gene Scheer, Mr. Picker ensures that these numbers enhance and give dimension to his characters — from Clyde Griffiths consumed by blinding ambition to grab his piece of the American dream and Thérèse Raquin's guilt-haunted conscience after the murder of her husband to Dolores Claiborne's moving attempt to explain her choices to her hardened daughter. "The words are another color for me," says Mr. Picker, whose settings take detailed account of the natural rhythms of language, thus bringing to mind another comparison that J.D. McClatchy has suggested: Janáček who similarly crafted indelible portraits of strong women "in a claustrophobic society."

Despite the unique sound world Mr. Picker constructs for each of these operas, they circle around recurrent shared themes: the struggle against repressive conventions, the situation of powerless but determined women, the illusion of religious consolation. Even the plot devices and settings of the literary sources on which he has drawn — from Theodore Dreiser and Emile Zola to Stephen King — contain uncanny echoes in their climactic scenes of drowning or trial. *Fantastic Mr. Fox*, based on the children's story by Roald Dahl, is an exception in being a comedy — but here, too, the comedy has a dark, sardonic edge, and the singing animals also serve an allegorical function as social commentary.

Yet for all the melodramatic, even Gothic, situations of his narratives, Mr. Picker's musical characterizations paint astute psychological portraits. Aria after aria in this collection shows him using the tools of his trade and the expressive power of the human voice to reveal a character's inner life or sense of self in the face of extreme situations. He might call for dramatic leaps in range to underscore Roberta Alden's desperation intensifying; or the high-lying vocal line of the murdered husband Camille come back as a ghost; or a sweet, resigned lyricism to depict lovesickness in "Miss Hedgehog's Aria" from *Fantastic Mr. Fox*. "Opera is about telling stories in music," emphasizes Mr. Picker. That's true not only across the large canvas of an entire opera but within the limits of an aria as well. For this composer, arias become a narrative microcosm and a key to character. As such, they call for skills both musical and dramatic from their interpreters, but the challenges posed by these pieces will give corresponding pleasure.

Thomas May
Author of *Decoding Wagner*
2014

Emmeline
(1996)
An opera in two acts
Libretto by J.D. McClatchy
Based on the novel by Judith Rossner
Commissioned by Santa Fe Opera

World Premiere: July 27, 1996: Santa Fe Opera
George Manahan, conductor
Francesca Zambello, director

Premiere Cast:
Emmeline Mosher: Patricia Racette (soprano)
Matthew Gurney: Curt Peterson (tenor)
Mr. Maguire: Victor Ledbetter (baritone)
Aunt Hannah Watkins: Anne-Marie Owens (dramatic contralto)
Henry Mosher: Kevin Langan (bass)
Sophie: Melanie Sarakatsannis (soprano)
Pastor Avery: Herbert Perry (bass)
Mrs. Bass: Josepha Gayer (mezzo-soprano)

Synopsis of *Emmeline*
by J.D. McClatchy

In mid-century rural Maine, 13-year-old Emmeline Mosher, the eldest child of a poor farming family, is sent to work at a textile mill. She is soon seduced by her married supervisor, becomes pregnant, and is dismissed from her job. Her aunt arranges to have the child—which Emmeline never sees—adopted. Twenty years later, back at home to care for her elderly parents, Emmeline falls in love with and marries a mysterious young stranger, Matthew Gurney. When her aunt comes to visit, it is revealed that Matthew is, in fact, her stolen child. Unable to bear the thought of losing both a husband and a son, Emmeline begs Matthew to stay, but he abandons her, disgusted. Emmeline is subsequently condemned and ostracized by the townspeople, but she bravely refuses to yield to others and resolves to stay put, triumphing in her very survival.

Based on a true story—and, more broadly, an Oedipal framework from Jocasta's point of view—*Emmeline* makes a heroine out of the unfortunate woman, reimagining events so that her inner life is given a moral shape. She is a powerful figure who seeks to free herself from the oppressive circumstances of the society she is part of—a society that denied women their share of passion and power, and demanded that religion control their actions. Picker's vivid, precisely orchestrated score proceeds deftly, never letting a scene outlast its welcome. The object of international acclaim, *Emmeline* is recognized as one of America's most important and successful operas of the second half of the twentieth century.

Fantastic Mr. Fox
(1998)
An opera in three acts
Libretto by Donald Sturrock
Based on the book by Roald Dahl
Originally commissioned to benefit the Roald Dahl Foundation (now Roald Dahl's Marvellous Children's Charity) with funding from Felicity Dahl.

World Premiere:
December 9, 1998; Los Angeles Opera
Peter Ash, conductor
Donald Sturrock, director

Premiere Cast:
Mr. Fox: Gerald Finley (baritone)
Mrs. Fox: Suzanna Guzmán (mezzo-soprano)
Farmer Boggis: Louis Lebherz (bass)
Farmer Bunce: Doug Jones (tenor)
Farmer Bean: Jamie Offenbach (bass-baritone)
Mavis the Tractor: Lesley Leighton (soprano)
Agnes the Digger: Jill Grove (mezzo-soprano)
Miss Hedgehog: Sari Gruber (soprano)
Badger the Miner: Malcolm MacKenzie (baritone)
Burrowing Mole: Jorge Garza (tenor)
Rita the Rat: Josepha Gayer (mezzo-soprano)
Porcupine: Charles Castronovo (tenor)

Synopsis of *Fantastic Mr. Fox*
by Donald Sturrock

Mr. Fox is the darling of the animals in the forest. He is clever, debonair and never at a loss for schemes to feed both family and friends. But he has enemies, and this time he may have met his match. A sinister trio of grotesque farmers, led by the evil Farmer Bean, will stop at nothing in their plans to destroy him and his family. The story of how the Foxes and their friends survive the farmers and their mechanical allies, Mavis the Tractor and Agnes the Digger, is a stirring one, yet it is one that is also filled with unexpected humour and edgy wit.

Based on one of the most popular stories of the celebrated children's author, Roald Dahl, *Fantastic Mr. Fox* is a tuneful, rhythmic work whose music is by turns funny, sad and frightening. Although Dahl's story is for children, Picker's opera operates at multiple levels of meaning, also serving as a modern fable about oppression and the struggles between good and evil and between mankind and nature. Since its premiere it has been revived in many new productions in the UK and USA, enchanting audiences of adults and children alike with its madcap energy and zany humor. Encompassing a variety of playful, catchy musical elements, including a love duet between a hedgehog and a porcupine as well as an unconventional fox-trot for the Foxes, the opera is guaranteed to appeal to anyone still youthful at heart.

Thérèse Raquin
(2001)
An opera in two acts
Libretto by Gene Scheer
Based on the novel by Émile Zola
Commissioned by The Dallas Opera, L'Opéra de Montréal and
The San Diego Opera

World Premiere:
November 30, 2001; Dallas Opera
Graeme Jenkins, conductor
Francesca Zambello, director

Premiere Cast:
Madame Lisette Raquin: Diana Soviero (soprano)
Thérèse Raquin: Sara Fulgoni (mezzo-soprano)
Camille Raquin: Gordon Gietz (tenor)
Laurent: Richard Bernstein (baritone)
Suzanne Michaud: Sheryl Woods (soprano)
Olivier Michaud: Gagor Andrasy (bass)
Monsieur Grivet: Peter Kazaras (tenor)

Synopsis of *Thérèse Raquin*
by Gene Scheer

Married Parisian couple Thérèse and Camille Raquin are reunited with an old friend, Laurent. It soon becomes clear that Thérèse and Laurent are more than old friends. Their intense passion stands in strong contrast to the loveless marriage that Camille and Therese have been enduring. Desperate to find a way of being together, Therese and Laurent conspire to drown Camille in the Seine. After the crime is committed the guilty couple begins a tragic descent, as they are tormented by their own consciences and the ghost of Camille.

For the plot to Picker's second opera, we have his sister, Ida Picker, to thank: she introduced Emile Zola's 1867 novel *Thérèse Raquin* to her brother after an old copy of the book fell off her bookshelf while dusting. The resulting opera proceeds with remarkable intensity, heightening the drama with its suspenseful and highly rhythmic score. Its music hovers between tonality and complex atonality, with the latter taking on a stronger role in the second act, as Thérèse and Laurent come to grips with their crime. Picker masterfully creates an intricate web of counterpoint via acrobatic vocal lines.

An American Tragedy
(2005)
Opera in Two Acts
Libretto by Gene Scheer
Based on the novel by Theodore Dreiser
Commissioned by The Metropolitan Opera

World Premiere:
December 2, 2005; The Metropolitan Opera
James Conlon, conductor
Francesca Zambello, director

Premiere Cast:
Roberta Alden: Patricia Racette (soprano)
Sondra Finchley: Susan Graham (mezzo-soprano)
Clyde Griffiths: Nathan Gunn (baritone)
Elvira Griffiths: Dolora Zajick (mezzo-soprano)
Elizabeth Griffiths: Jennifer Larmore (mezzo-soprano)
Samuel Griffiths: Kim Begley (tenor)
Gilbert Griffiths: William Burden (tenor)
Orville Mason: Richard Bernstein (baritone)
Hortense: Anna Christy (soprano)

Synopsis of *An American Tragedy*
by Gene Scheer

Clyde Griffiths, a poor, Midwestern missionary's 20-year-old son takes a job in his affluent uncle's factory in upstate New York. Clyde soon rises to the position of foreman and is warned of a no fraternization policy between management and staff. Despite this warning, Clyde pursues a factory worker named Roberta Alden. As this relationship is developing, Clyde is introduced to the socialite world of his uncle's children. After spending a night with Roberta, Clyde begins a romantic relationship with Sondra Finchley, the beautiful daughter of one of the town's industrialists. When Clyde plans to break off the relationship with Roberta to pursue this new romance, he discovers that Roberta is pregnant. Clyde schemes to rid himself of his unwanted lover with a child on the way.

An adaptation of Theodore Dreiser's novel by the same name, *An American Tragedy* is a progressive drama of temptation, responsibility, and faith that ponders a common dilemma at the heart of the American experience: in this land of hope and boundless promise, how do we find the balance between our moral duties and our quest for the American dream? These questions live in the space between every note of Picker's powerfully meticulous work, and while searching for their answers, he has spun them into melodies that capture the optimism, sorrow and frailty of Clyde Griffith's "Everyman."

Dolores Claiborne
(2013)
An opera in two acts
Libretto by J.D. McClatchy
Based on the novel by Stephen King
Commissioned by San Francisco Opera

World Premiere:
September 18, 2013; San Francisco, CA
George Manahan, conductor
James Robinson, director

Premiere Cast:
Dolores Claiborne: Patricia Racette (soprano) / Catherine Cook (mezzo-soprano)
Vera Donovan: Elizabeth Futral (soprano)
Joe St. George: Wayne Tigges (bass-baritone)
Selena St. George: Susannah Biller (soprano)
Detective Thibodeau: Greg Fedderly (tenor)

Synopsis of *Dolores Claiborne*
by J.D. McClatchy

The opera opens with an interrogation, police officers accusing Dolores Claiborne of murdering the rich and imperious Vera Donovan, who employed Dolores as a maid and companion for forty years. As Dolores answers the officers' questions, we learn how her difficult marriage ended in the murder of her depraved husband, who had been sexually molesting their teen-age daughter. It is then revealed that Vera and Dolores were close friends, and that Vera left her entire fortune to Dolores. Even after learning of her innocence in Vera's death, Dolores's emotionally fraught daughter cannot forgive her mother—and even though Dolores has done everything a mother and woman can to keep three lives together, ultimately she is left alone.

Based on the best-selling novel by Stephen King, *Dolores Claiborne* is one of the most compelling characters to emerge from the esteemed writer's imagination. Passionate, desperate, trapped, the feisty Maine house-keeper will do anything to save the daughter who despises her. Dolores is a natural fit for opera—specifically for Picker's dark theatricality. *Dolores Claiborne* is Picker's fifth opera, a musical and dramatic triumph.

About the Arias

Emmeline

You Can See The Farm From Here
Character: Matthew
Setting: A clearing with a view near the Mosher family farm, Fayette, Maine (1861)
Against her father's wishes, Emmeline has accepted Matthew's marriage proposal. Matthew shows her the view from the site upon which he will build their house. He says he can see their bright future: "All for you, all for me!"

Fantastic Mr. Fox

Farmer Bunce's Aria
Character: Farmer Bunce
Setting: The decrepit farmyards of Boggis, Bunce, and Bean
Farmer Bunce, the Francophile, explains his obsession with geese.

Thérèse Raquin

The Seine Moves Like A Melody*
Character: Camille
Setting: The Raquin home, Passage du Pont Neuf, Paris
The sickly Camille poetically describes the Seine, in an effort to persuade his mother to allow him to go for a riverside walk and picnic with Thérèse and Laurent.

Ghost Aria
Character: Camille
Setting: Madame Raquin's bedroom in the Raquin home, Passage du Pont Neuf, Paris
Camille comes to his mother in a dream describing his drowning murder at the hands of Laurent and Thérèse.

An American Tragedy

Car Aria**
Character: Clyde Griffiths
Setting: Samuel Griffiths' shirt factory, Lycurgus, New York
Clyde watches as his rich cousin Gilbert drives off in a fancy car. He is filled with envious determination to have a car of his own and to lead the life of a rich man one day.

Drunk Aria
Character: Gilbert Griffiths, Clyde's rich cousin
Setting: Lycurgus, New York during Bella Griffiths' birthday party
Gilbert belittles his poor cousin Clyde, humiliating him in front of the Lycurgus high society Clyde longs to join.

* In the version currently in use this aria is sung by Olivier (bass). In the original version of the opera this aria was sung by Camille (tenor).

** In the opera this aria is performed by a baritone.

You Can See The Farm From Here

from "Emmeline"

J.D. McClatchy

Tobias Picker

♩ = 96–120

ff

mp

MATTHEW: *jaunty*

You can see the farm from here. You can see the hills right clear. There's Ken - ne - bec and Port - land Har - bor. You can see the whole state of Maine! You can see the fu -

8vb

-ture! The sky's put out his_____ big blue

hand._____ The trees all want to ex - plain.

You can see___ the fu - ture here!_____ It's_

_____ all blue and green!_____ It's all o - pen and free.

All for you,____ all for me!____

Noth - ing, noth - ing is the same.____ You were-n't a - live then. You

just came a - live right here, right now.__ You've_ giv - en

such a life____ to me.____ Books and feel - ings,

a ten - der - ness, such___ a sense of be - ing home that I want to build

a house for us. You can see___ the fu - ture here.___ I'll

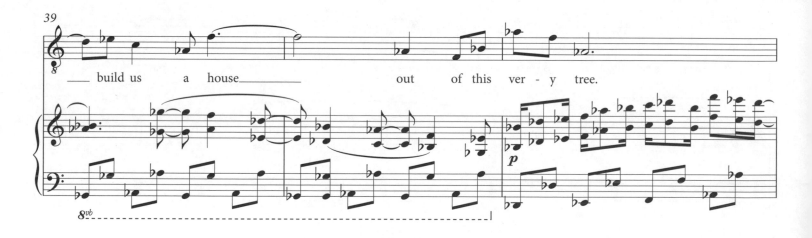

___ build us a house___ out of this ver - y tree.

Em - me - line,___ come to me!___

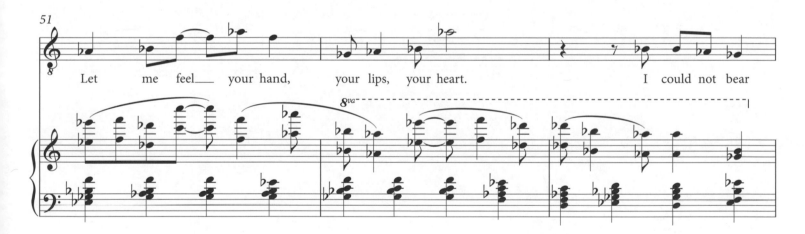

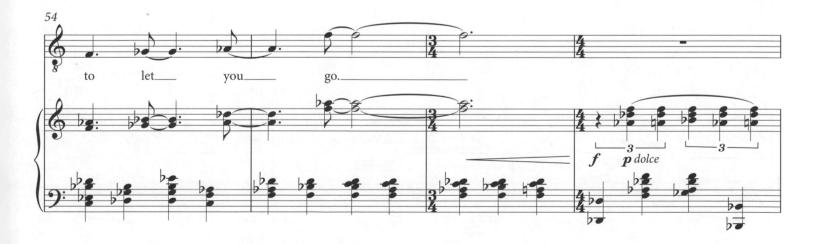

I could nev - er let you__ go.__

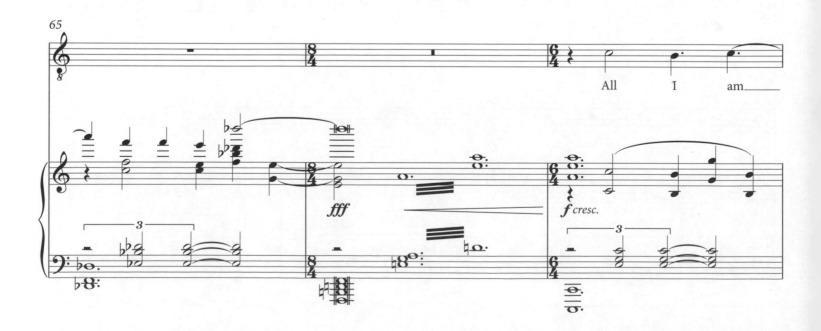

All I am__

is yours.　　　All　I was, all　I　am,　all　I　can be,　I　am yours.

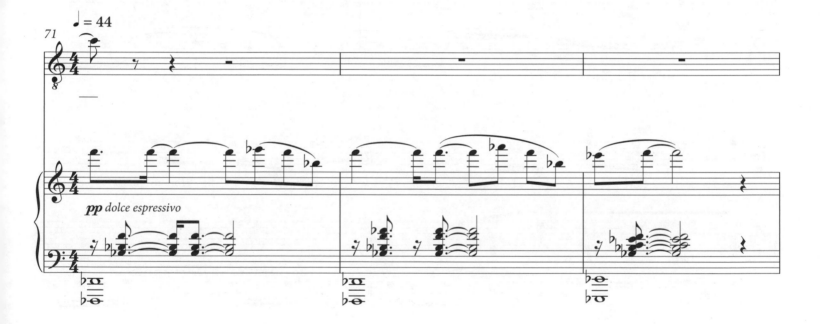

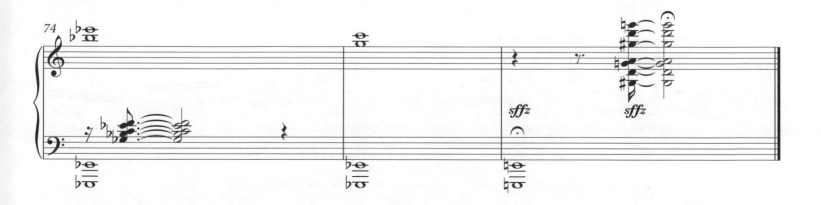

Farmer Bunce's Aria
from "Fantastic Mr. Fox"

Donald Sturrock

Tobias Picker

ED 30135

bas - es   the   art   of   good   food!

I've   con - sult - ed   all   the   fin - est chefs   a - cook - ing

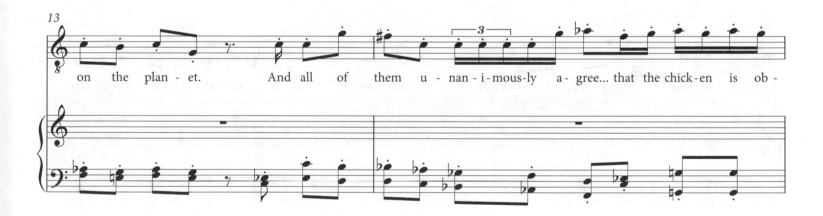

on   the   plan - et.   And   all   of   them   u - nan - i - mous-ly   a - gree... that the chick-en   is   ob -

nox-ious.   In   a   per-fect world you'd ban   it.   *(Putting on a French accent)*   And   it's   a great shame that the on - ly ones who see   are the

to the goose! The food of roy - al - ty the fowl of kings!

Hail to the goose! The bird the French a - dore. The or - i - gin of foie gras and

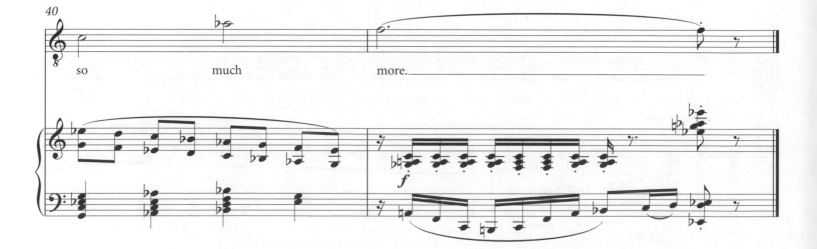

so much more.

The Seine Moves Like A Melody
from "Thérèse Raquin"

Gene Scheer

Tobias Picker

ED 30135

own u-nique de - sign.   He says it   moves un - ex - pect-ed - ly   as if

God had turned   his head   and   let   the   gen - tle

riv - er___   lead the way   in - stead.   You must let   me go   Ma-

ma.   My ill - ness now   has passed.

Let me move on like the riv-er. I am strong e-nough at

last. Ma-

ma, it will be such fun. Now, don't___ say a word...

___ but yes! Ma-ma... Ma-ma...___

rit.

Ghost Aria
from "Thérèse Raquin"

Gene Scheer

Tobias Picker

Ghost Aria

Allegro, poco pesante ♩ = 96–120

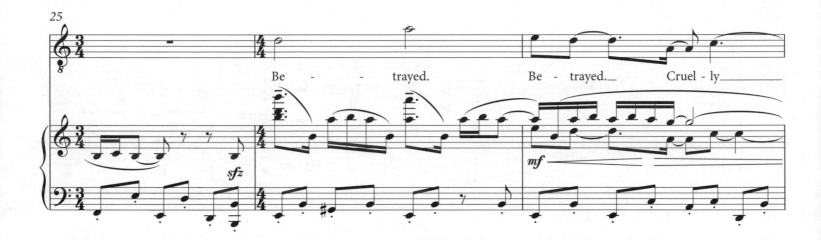

Hear me. Hear me. Hear me. Your Ca-mille is next to you now.____ My breath____

____ is____ the breeze____ that moist-ens your brow.

My breath____ is the breeze____ that mois -

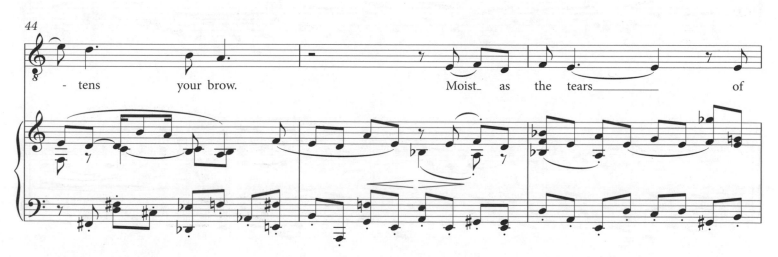

- tens your brow. Moist_ as the tears____ of

an-guish you cried__ when you learned your on - ly son__ had died.____

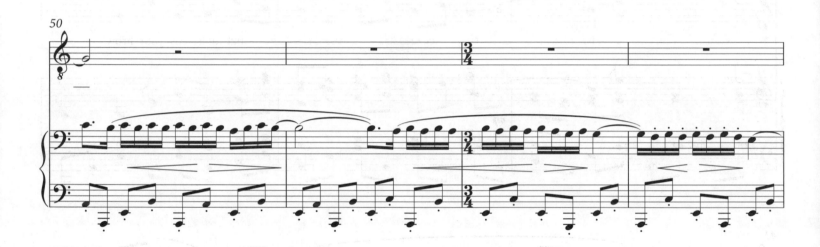

Died!_____

Cruel - ly,____ cruel - ly____ be - - trayed.____

____ Be - trayed!____ Be-trayed by those we loved.____ Moth-er, lis-ten.

Moth-er, lis - ten. The riv - - er's____ plain - tive__ mel - o -

dy has turned in - to my__ el - - - e - gy,____ my__ el - e - gy.

I _____ called, "Thé-rèse," _____ looked in her eyes, _____

_____ and _____ saw _____ a _____ face _____ I _____

_____ did _____ not _____ rec - og - nize.

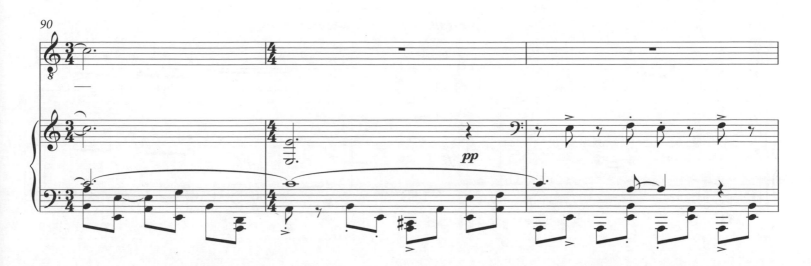

pp

Touch me. Touch me. Moth - er, touch me. Touch me. Touch me. Feel me. Feel

me. Feel my em - brace._____ I__ am the_____ shad - ow__ veil -

- ing__ your face._____ Dark__ as a soul_____ that__ can__

nev - er be__ saved.__ Dark as_____ the depths of__

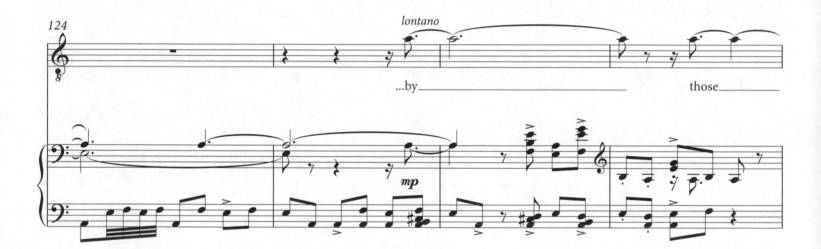

Car Aria
from "An American Tragedy"

Gene Scheer

Tobias Picker

CLYDE:

A mo-tor car!___ There he goes!

What a car! What a car! What a beau-ti-ful car. Bur-gun-dy red with wood-en trim.

What would it be like be-ing him?___ Driv-ing to din-ner,___ to dance with

ED 30135

Car Aria

friends. The car twists like a smile___ as the road___ bends.___

Ar - riv - ing!___ There I go! The hum of the en - gine still in my

veins. A hum that sings what I've al-ways known, my fu-ture as bright as pol-ished chrome.___

Car Aria

But look at me now! Fif - teen a

week and run-ning this floor!_ Hard work_ and hope.___ A few years_ from now___

_ I can_ see it: more!_____

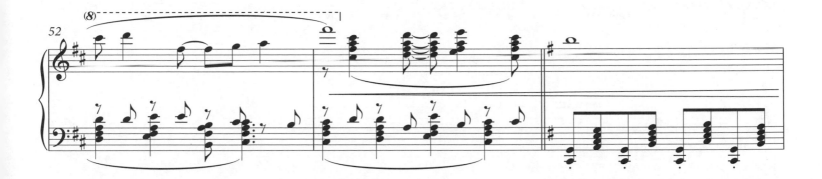

That pret-ty girl._ What was her name? I be-lieve, I be-lieve, yes, Ro-ber-ta, that's

right! When she spoke to her friend, she looked at me. "The Em-pire at eight, un-der the mar-quee!"

I'm driv-ing to din-ner___ to dance with friends. The car

twists like a smile___ as the road___ bends. Oh, to sit___

___ be-hind___ the___ wheel___ and___ feel noth - ing___

___ but ease___ as I climb each hill.___ Grav-i-ty___ can't...

Grav - i - ty_____ can't hold_ me still._____

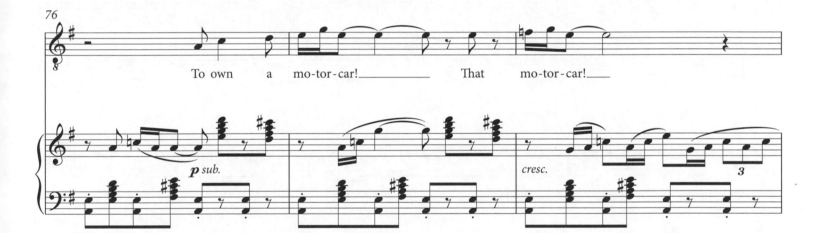

To own a mo-tor-car!_____ That mo-tor-car!___

Bur - gun - dy red with wood-en trim!_____

Drunk Aria
from "An American Tragedy"

Gene Scheer

Tobias Picker

It's true. It's true. Ask him. It's true. I'm sure he'll tell you it's true. All the

new danc-es come from Chi-ca - go. All the new danc-es come from Chi-ca- go.

He's from Chi-ca - go. He must know Will-iam Thomp- son? Of course he knows him!

He worked at his fa - ther's__ ho -tel!__ He must love their place on Lake Mich-i- gan.

28

Fa-ther says that it is twice the size of our homes up-state.

31 ♩ = 60 ♩ = 90 ♩ = 72

Gin__ en-hanc-es my man-y charms. My man-y charms are en-hanced.__

34

I can see games be-ing__ played by pret-ty rich girls. Here's to pret-ty rich

38

girls!__